CARTOON CHARACTER CARS
COLORING BOOK

Check out heydanievera.com for more products!
Share your work **#heydanielvera** on social media

AN AUTHOR'S NOTE FOR A FUTURE ARTIST

Thank you very much for purchasing my book!
I really value your support and hope you have a lot of fun.

I have dedicated half of my life to drawing, painting and designing cars.

One day I thought about making a coloring book about cars that I would have
liked to have been given when I was your age, but for some reason something
like that didn't exist. So I said, why not do it?

I hope you enjoy each piece of art in this book as much as I enjoyed making it,
so I look forward to seeing your finished masterpieces.

Please tag @heydanielvera or use #heydanielvera

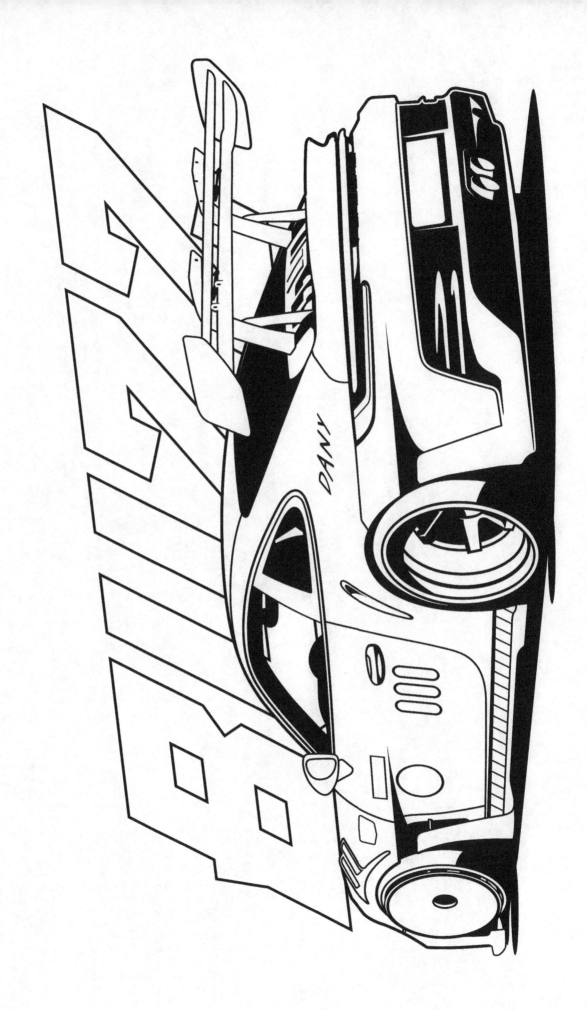

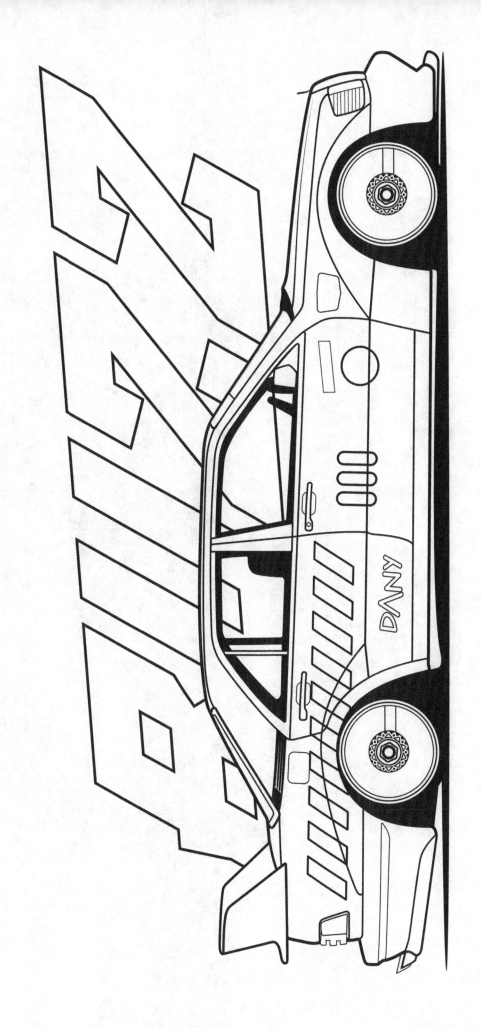

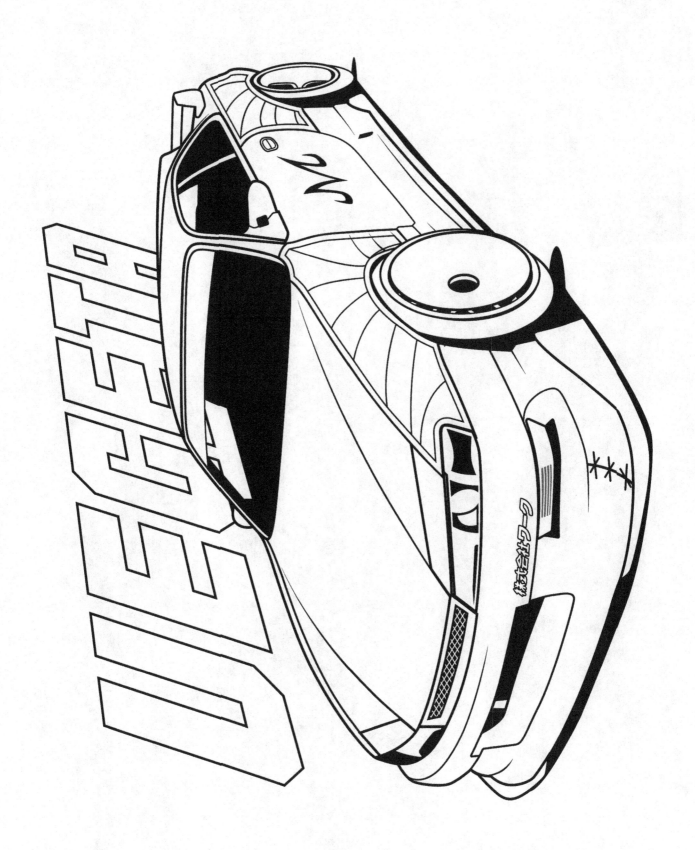

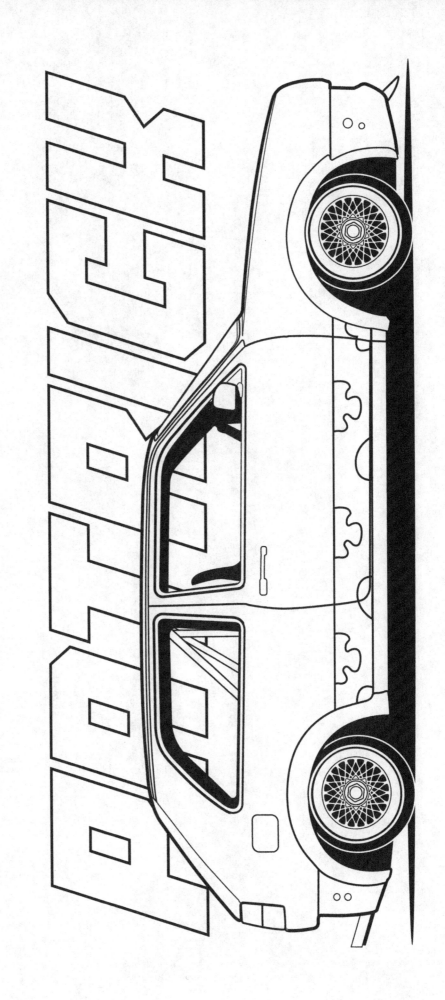

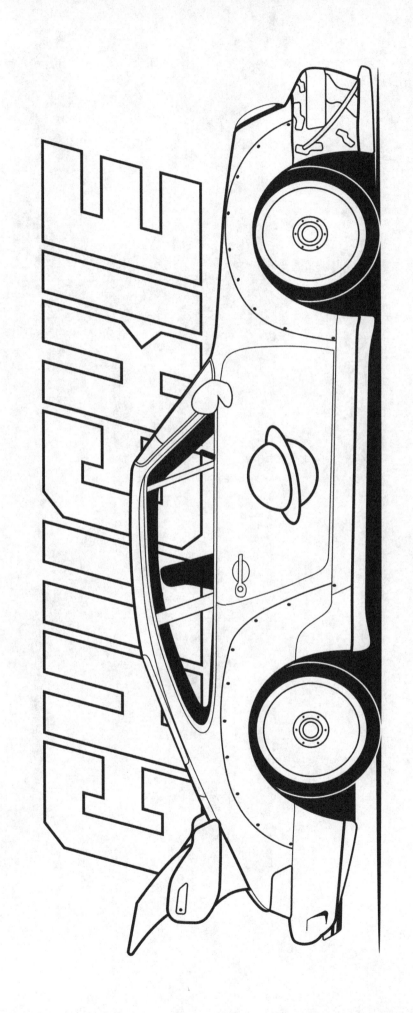

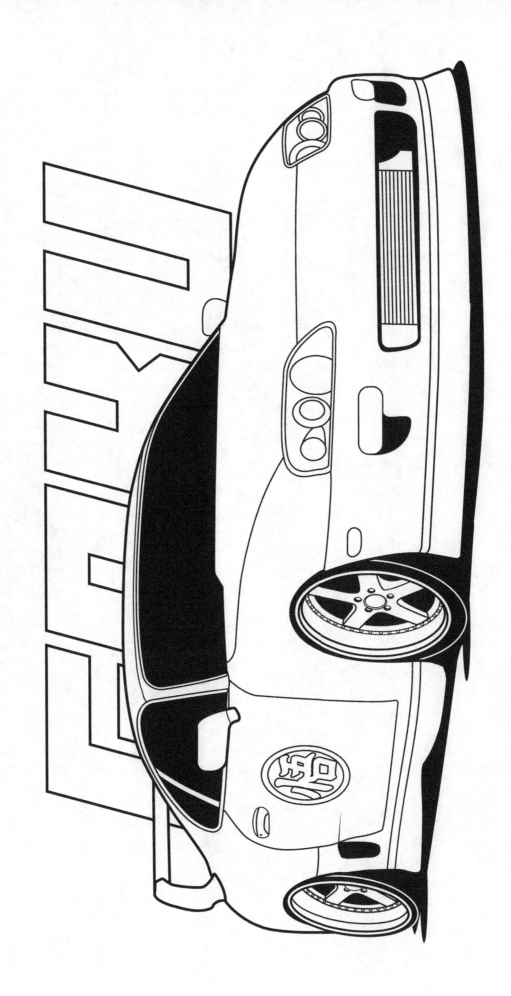

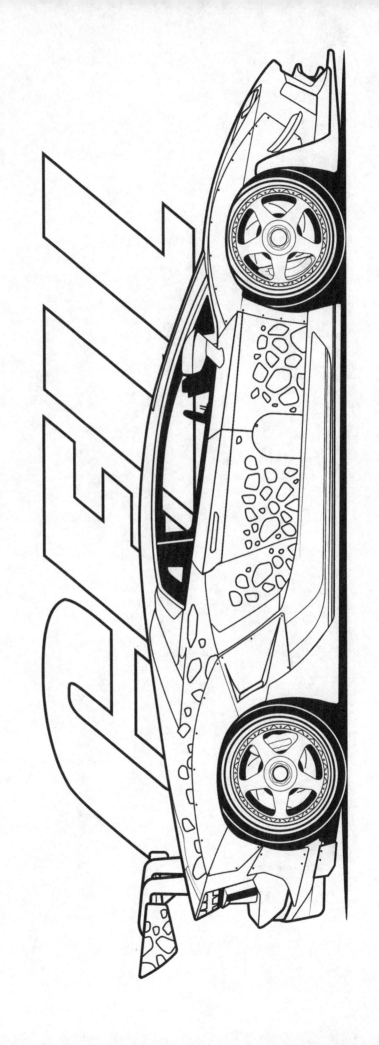

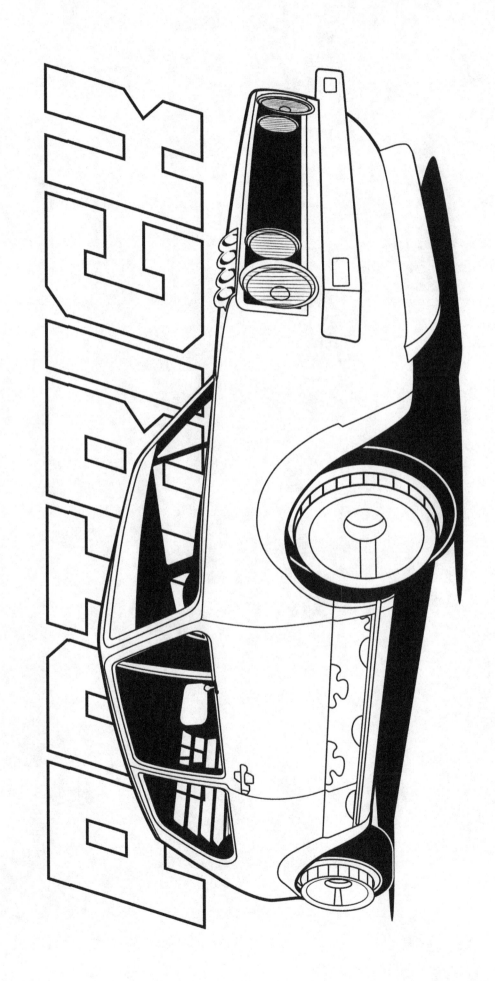

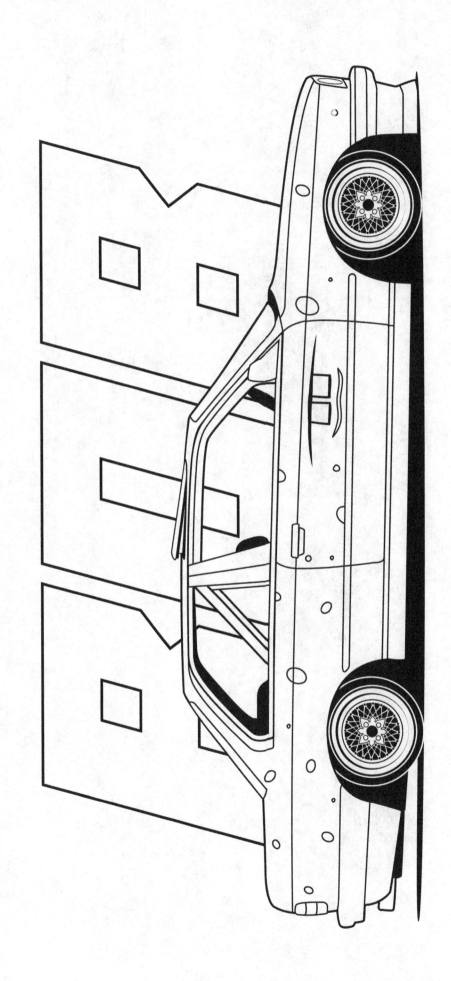

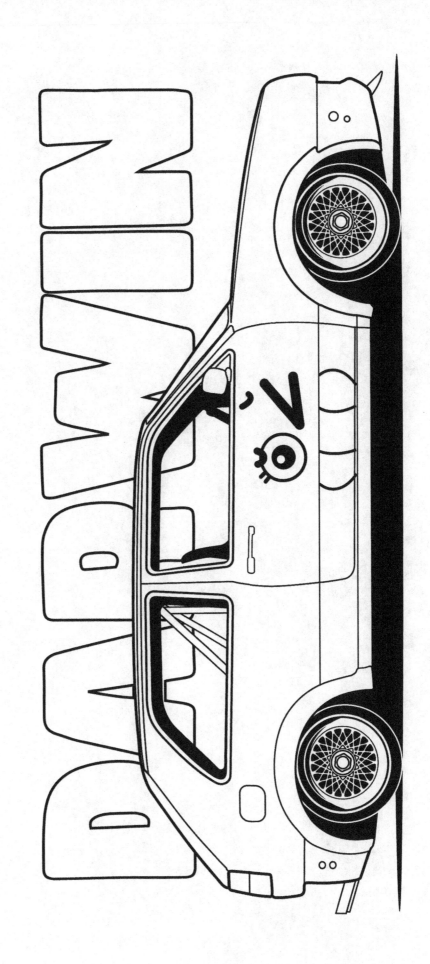

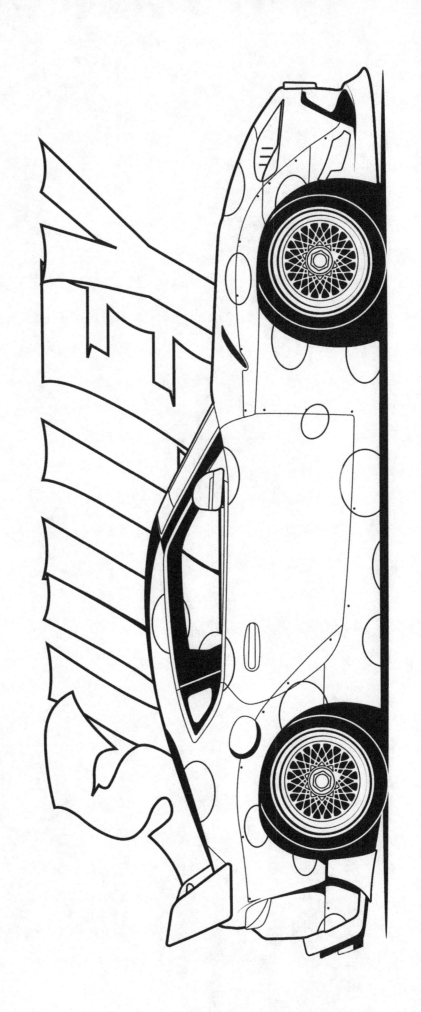

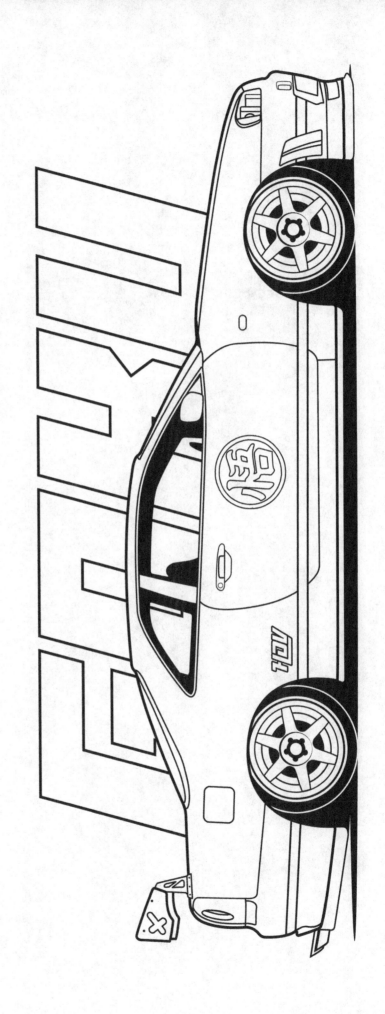

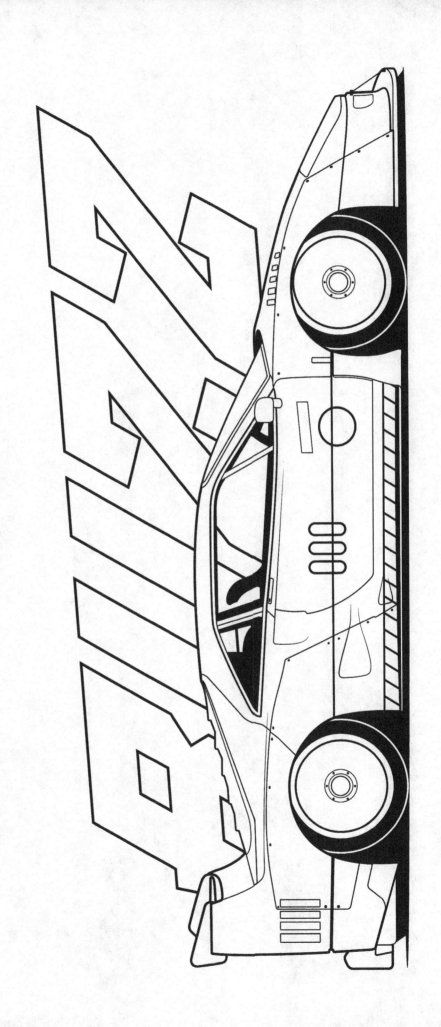

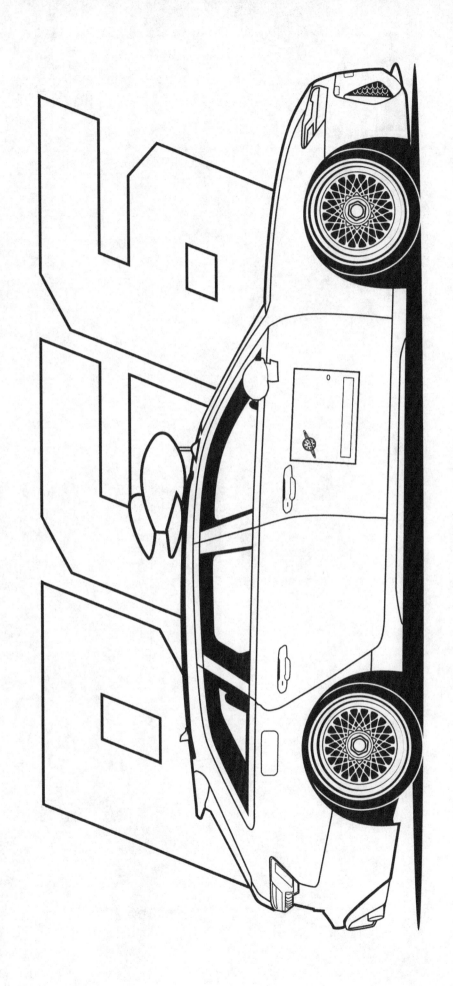

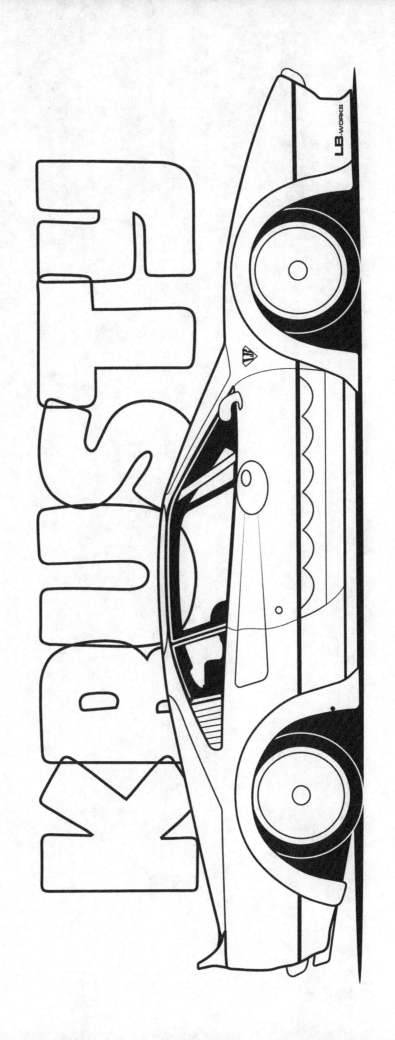

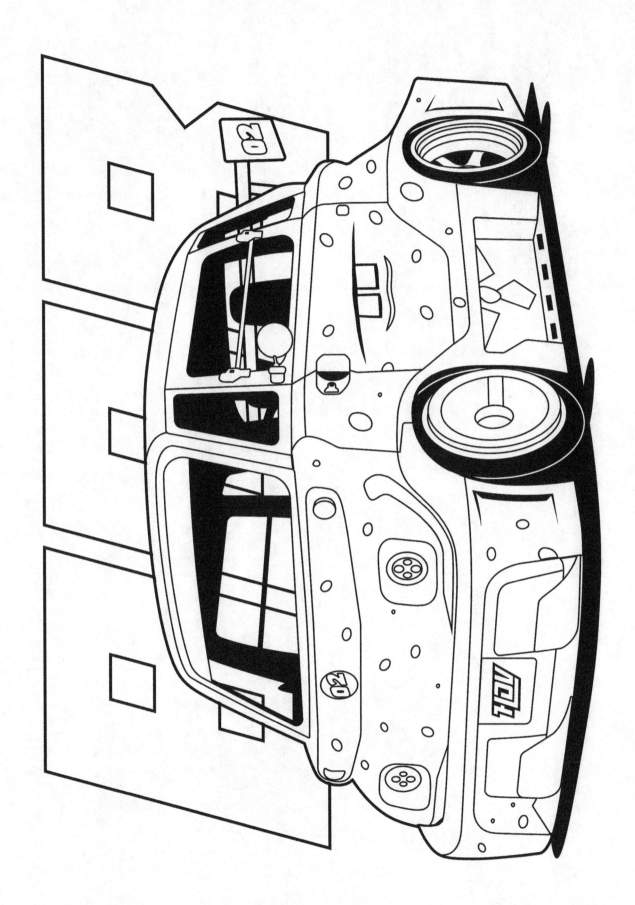

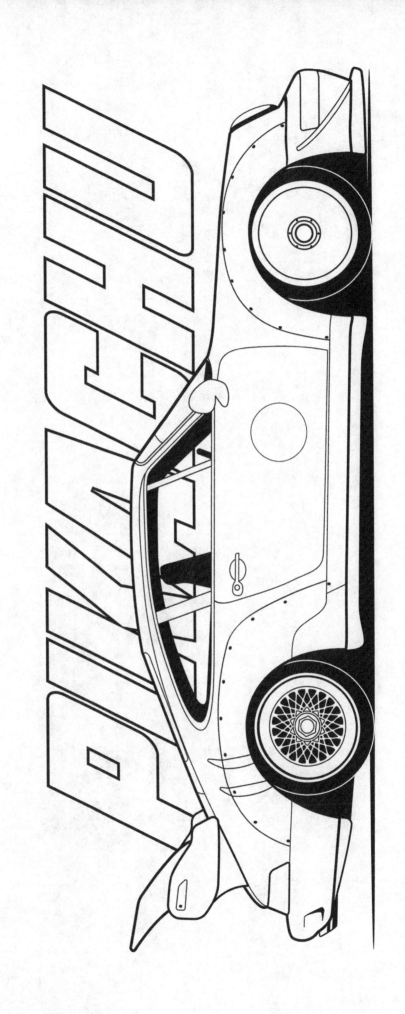

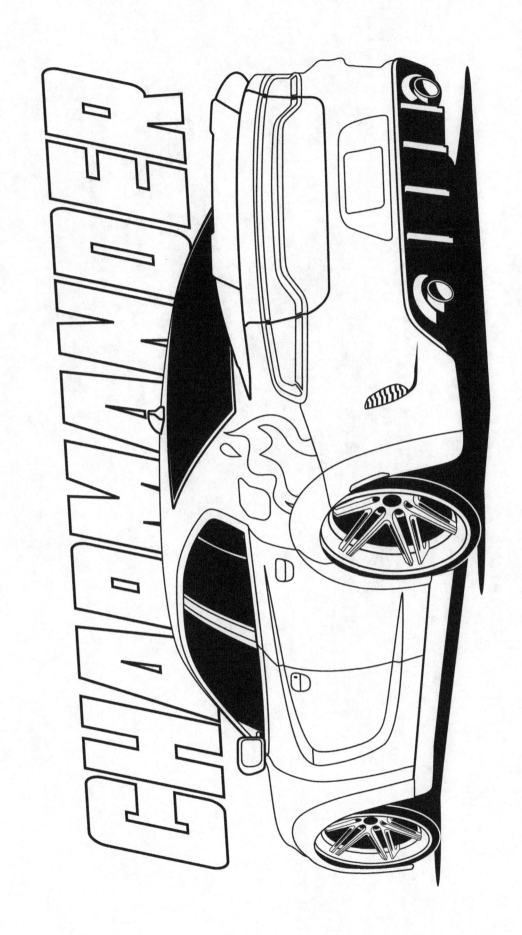

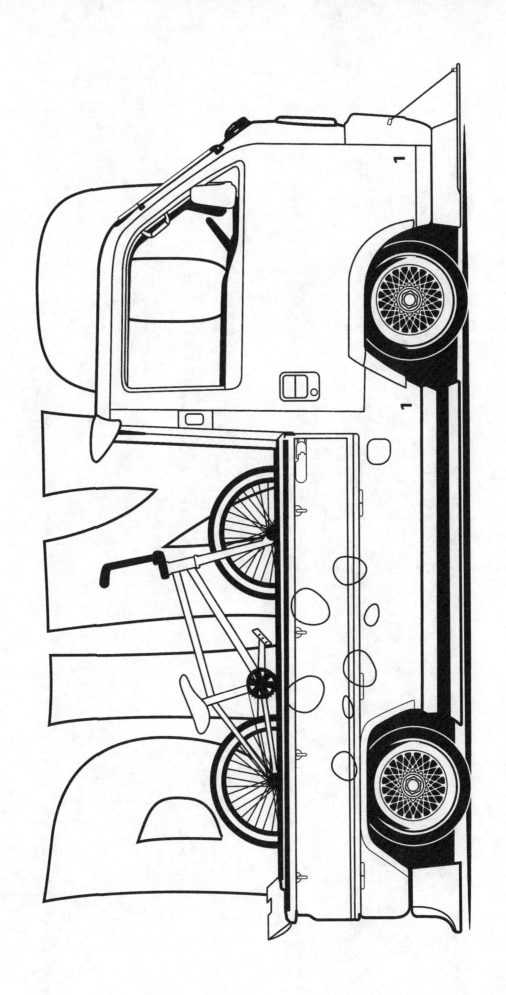

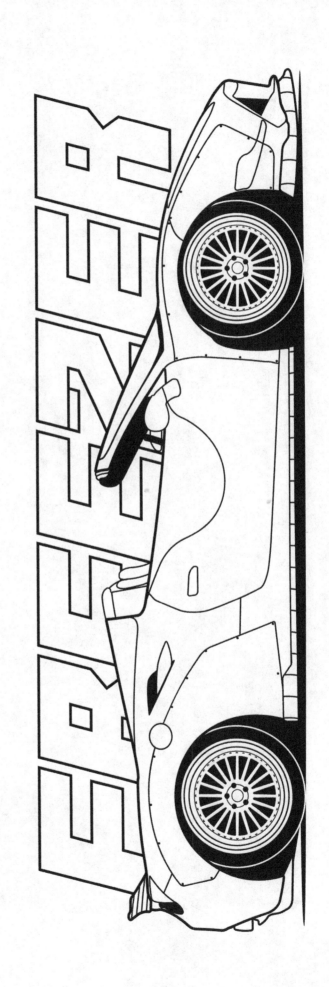

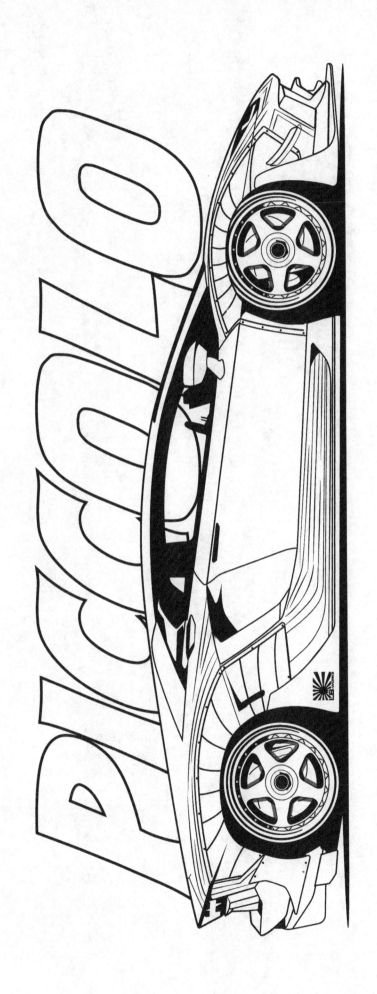

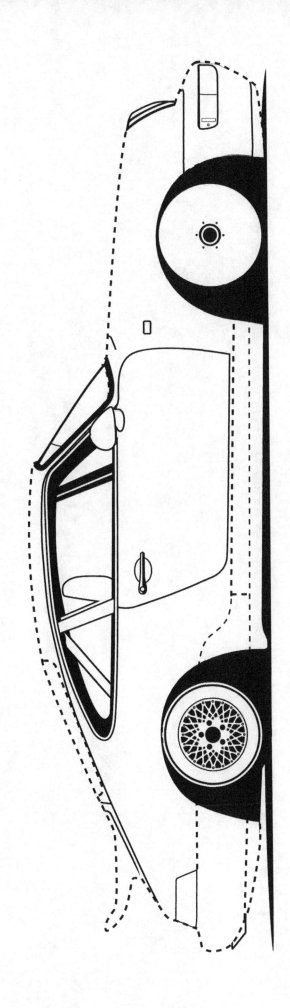

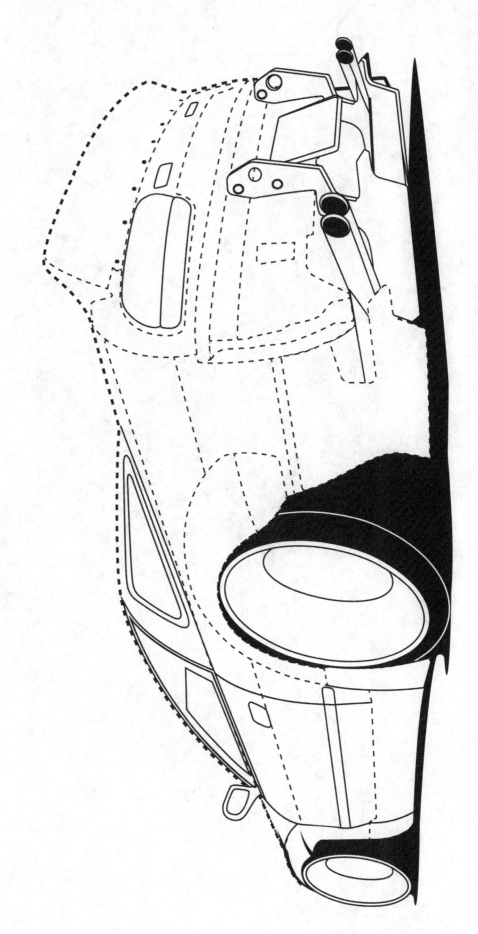

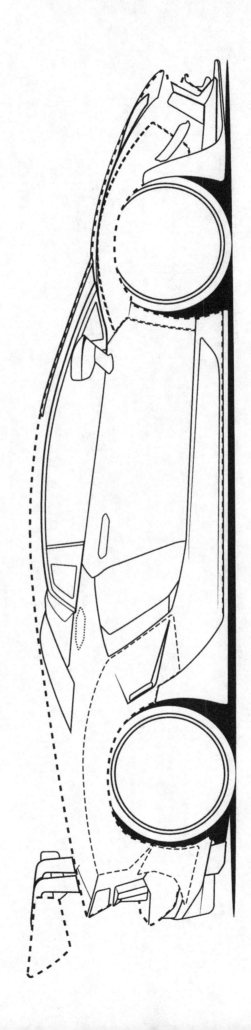

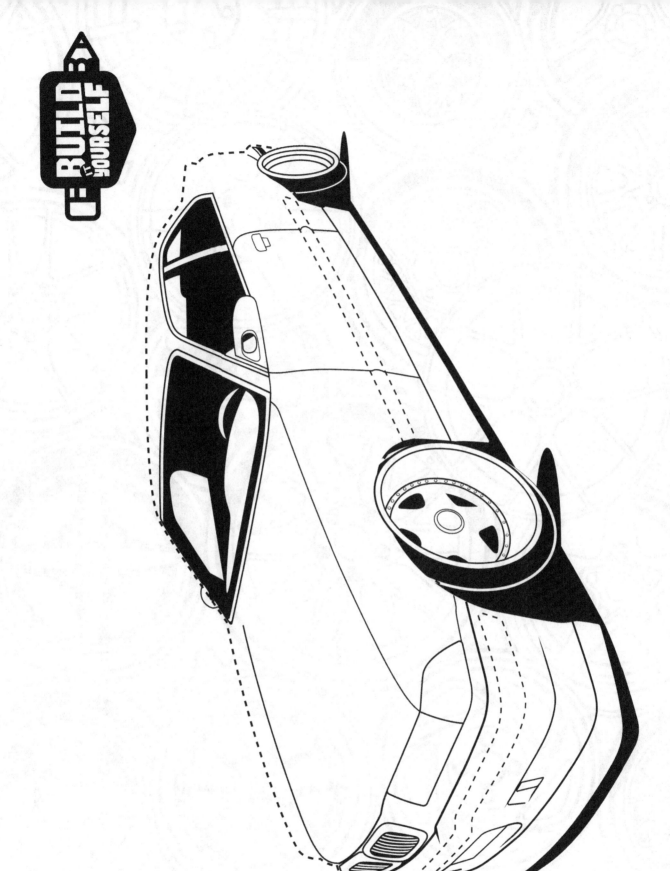

BUILD YOURSELF

WWW.HEYDANIELVERA.COM

Made in the USA
Columbia, SC
19 April 2024

34586040R00050